Rise

Echoes of Healing and Hope

John Bjorgaard

Copyright © 2023 John Bjorgaard

All rights reserved.

Illustrations by Shayla Sackinger

Second Edition

Rise

Echoes of Healing and Hope

John Bjorgaard

Table of Contents

Echoes of Healing and Hope 2

Vices 5

Ignorant Bliss 6

I Am Fine 7

Ritual of Destruction 8

Nightmare 9

Break Me 10

Reality 11

Counting Quarters 12

Consequence 13

Throne 14

Day One 15

Rise 17

Kinder 18

Stained Glass 19

Neverland 20

Never too Late 21

Solitude 22

Better Place 23

Stronger 24

Love Me 26

Comfort 27

Bloom 28

Therapy 29

Progress 30

Vices

Caving a lot recently to my vices

When did these walls turn to sand

I can't remember the last time I checked prices

For these coping tools in my hand

A pint, a pitcher, maybe a bottle to share

Anything to turn down the silent scolding

Eyes aimed down with the blankest stare

Knowing full well it's not a drink I should be holding

It should be conversations

It should be the people I love

Not these temporary relieving sensations

As the glasses are lifted above

My head filled with these empty ideas

My chest heaving, my heart blind

These are the nights of silent pleas

The nights I'll do anything to quiet my mind

Ignorant Bliss

I used to love the tingle you brought

The confidence given away in the excess

Forgetting the hardest lessons you taught

In the moments I feel the most worthless

I learned your impacts cracked the foundation

Staining the lens of my world view

But when overcome with frustration

Somehow the path always leads back to you

Ignoring the faults the way I would a text

Begging for you to take away the hurt

Sprinting past the numb, knowing what's next

No inhibitions, no judgement to assert

Only dulled senses and the blissful void

Before dreams of milestones starting to fall

Waking to find another life destroyed

By who I thought was my friend, alcohol

I Am Fine

I'm not tired, just had a long night
You don't need to worry about me it's only wine
You can dig and pry with all your might
I'm not opening up, I Am Fine

I never asked you to be there for me
I'd rather just be left alone
Then become a burden on your curiosity
Then be questioned about my lack of tone

Pushing, clawing, fighting for space
I just need a glass to let my emotions steep
Not caring how many it takes to reach the quiet place
Stop being scared for me, I'm just trying to sleep

Ritual of Destruction

No fruit for me please, I drink my pain neater than most

Junipers familiar caress as the gin touches my lips

Won't you join me in this ritual of self destruction with a toast

I promise the speech will be worth it, I've memorized the scripts

Through years of repetition this detonation has been impending

With masterful muscle memory the glass touches down

Drinking like the world could be ending

Now you know why my name has weight in this town

Its not the heft of pride or prestige

But one of an anchor long separated from its chain

Dragging those around me down into the deep

Boisterous and volatile spreading my personal pain

Please know the cycle will end with my blood

I've shed it to many times to let it continue to draw breath

And even if I end up drowning in the ensuing flood

This black hole of addiction will not transcend my death

Nightmare

Flashing lights in the rearview mirror
Regret comes washing over you
A raging torrent of whiskey and beer
Embarrassed, nervous, lucky, all true

Fortunate for the life saved that night
Blessed by fate to have been caught
Deep down knowing it wasn't right
Overwhelmed for a moment with the pain you could've brought

Mistakes are a human trait
You've begged and pleaded to take it back
But in the end, I hold no presence of hate
 Freely offering help getting a life back on track

I was lucky, shuddering with the memory
Tilting my head back to scream
Consumed by the night now behind me
Living it again stuck in a daydream

Break Me

Break me
Take the pieces that you need
Build yourself, into all that you can be
I'll fix until I'm broken, this is my creed

Don't mind my grinding gears
I've got more than one screw loose
But onward I March through these years
Endlessly replacing every blown fuse

Collapse my lungs if you desire
Claim the beating of my very heart
Throw my body upon the pyre
If only to keep you and the cold apart

If keeping you warm is the last act
Of my scrapheap mortal coil
I'll take solace that I've made an impact
As my ashes settle into the soil

Reality

I would trade every ounce of creativity
For a glimpse beyond the veil
Take everything that makes me
Another statistic, a nameless white male

I don't need my name
But does the universe have a use for anxiety?
I could deliver a triple shipment
If only it were that easy to unload my instability

What is the point? Why am I here?
Questions that will seemingly forever lay unanswered
Whispers stuck in the fresh paint of my mind
Another distraction to cover the murals that drive me to the edge

Take my creations, I've thrown them into the void
Begging the universe to look at me
Spending my recreational moments trying to avoid
Reality

Counting Quarters

Another week stretching the last quarter as far as it will go
Counting them out across the sticky bar top
A watching man fills the room with remorse
Proudly informing the bartender not to stop

"His next glass is on me!"
Great
Another debt I will never be able to pay
Piling my quarters back into that crusted ashtray

Another *Blessing* given for free
Another soul with something over me
A whispered "poor man"
Another night wishing it was my last one
Knowing full well how many quarters are back in my pocket

To be counted out across that epoxy again
Rinsing and repeating the comfort until it no longer consoles
Repeating the destruction until it destroys the man
And leaves my heart full of holes

Consequence

Embracing sin was to let you in
Acting without consequence was letting you stay
Here in the darkness, I now begin
Forever alone for allowing you a day

Throne

So many nights I've asked the same thing
What the fuck is wrong with me?
Senses hanging on by a shoestring
Doing things over and over, insanity

Getting so caught up in being alone
Overwhelmed by my own emotional misuse
Kneeling before this metaphorical throne
Built from the ground up with my substance abuse

These bad habits, I've lived under their rule
Given away every illusion of choice
There is no ruler half as cruel
That the one that steals your consciences' voice

I've done day one again, and again
Motivated by others artwork
I'll do it over and over, I am not insane!
I'll keep doing day one every time, until my time to rule

Day One

I am so tired of my own apologies

Wanting so bad to disconnect my brain

This life I've got is full of amazing realities

I need to focus on those instead of past pain

When it's dark and it's cold I catch myself

Scurrying for tunnels I know well

Exchanging my worth for anything on the shelf

Wake up next to regret head pounding like hell

The turmoil of hurt and pain I know the cycle

Living through it once I should know better now

What a legacy I'm leading for Michael

I'm done feeling shitty staring at the ground

This is going to happen quietly I suppose

This being a little promise to me

It shouldn't matter to me who else knows

Today marks day one of sobriety

Rise

Community, it is what joins us
How am I to know you without history?
After my introduction, I'm supposed to blindly trust?
An addiction and a name
No
There is so much more to me

A mistake I made has shaped my future
Directed my steps towards light
I didn't need your help!
I'm not a moocher
I had to exist in that darkness
To find my bright
It took me so long to learn

We are all here
For a common growth
We are not hopeless
Cast out those lies
Every meeting leaves me reveling
In our common oath
From this low, I know we will Rise

Kinder

Admitting when I've made mistakes

Has grown something beautiful

Accountability

A tree ripe with lesson's fruit

Each a memory

Each a reminder

Of the hardest things life has taught me

A blooming billboard reminds me to be kinder

To myself

Stained Glass

Broken pieces of color scattered across my table
Individual fragments of the past, each with a history
Trying to arrange them, to keep them stable
Could I maybe hold together a picture unique to me?

No filing the rough edges away
Finding the points that fit together neat
Taking what the world has broken and choosing to create
From the wreckage, a place for my heart to weep

If beauty can be built from the broken
I'll hold out hope for the working class
No words need to be spoken
Admiring the morning sun through stained glass

Neverland

It must be the middle of the night

Alone with my mind, it's fight or flight

Headphones gripping my skull tight

Pen in hand, time to write

Crafting tapestries woven out of dreams

Weaving a silence from deafening screams

Pulling the fabric tight, checking the seams

Maybe this bag will hold the weight of theses reams.

I'll need to make the shoulder straps strong

The path to the waking world is long

I have to resist the lost boys' siren song

Living in neverland would surely be wrong

Never too Late

How do you deal with words that won't stop flying

Ambitions and dreams sprouting without direction

How old was I before realizing some of them were dying

What used to be my life goals leaving a cold empty reflection

On the days when the volume inside is cranked too high

I've floundered with those moments since I can remember

A hurting young man, a weary old soul, too young to suffer and too old to cry

The fire of creativity that roared within reduced to a mere ember

But in the ensuing darkness, that dull glow burns bright

The north star of the compass inside my soul

Bathing old obsessions in its soft warm light

This flame burning up inside of me, for the first time I feel whole

Rekindled is the desire to improve, to create

Roaring internally is the hammer on the anvil of my heart

Whenever you're overwhelmed, just know its never to late

And what's most important is the courage to start

Solitude

I have never felt more alone

Than when deserted by my own mind

Searching for sanity and learning none has grown

The seeds didn't get planted while I was focused on the grind

In the moments I need an answer, a reason to keep going

That's when I notice the empty baggage I've been keeping close

The weight I now understand being the reason I keep slowing

Crushing my resolve as my brain devolves into throes

Is being alone supposed to be freedom or a curse

I know a day will come when the answer will emerge

An epiphany landing atop the hearse

In the final moment when all the loneliness meets the purge

While biding my time before that impending day

I'll do my best to look back on all that I've accrued

Making my best effort to find any reason to stay

Even if the journey traps me in a state of solitude

Better Place

How much will this world take from you?

Wandering, floating through the nothingness.

How does your aura remain such a vibrant hue?

Brightening my day with your every bless

Maybe the world isn't done taxing your shine

But I don't think that will stop you from giving

To every soul you meet

Something Divine

Spreading happiness unto the world just by living

I've heard the ways are mysterious

When navigating the treacherous pathway towards grace

I hope you know I'm quite serious

When saying "You make the world a better place"

Stronger

Has being different always been akin to a bullseye on your shirt?

Does it bother you that much when my brain takes a little longer

Awake but never alone, just me and this hurt

When I imagined building character, I looked stronger

Solace amongst those that tolerate my company

I promise the smile beaming is nothing less than sincere.

Surrounded by those that love me for me

If only I could see what they do, looking in the mirror

The order of words has long amazed my brain

Memories woven amongst current events

Without that glimpse of love, would I know the hurt of pain?

Question after question living this life in the past tense

Who has time to worry about tomorrow

When right now has everything I could ever need

I'm done giving this worry my sorrow

My friends planted worth within me, I'm watering this seed

Love Me

I wish the wounds your words left showed clearly on my skin

Perhaps then you'd realize my silence isn't disrespect

It is pain

It severed my tongue, leaves me choking on all the things I haven't said

I wish the scars of my mind were apparent to the naked eye

Memories given form; stories tattooed by life's needle, I just want to see them

To remember I am art, more than an easel

On nights like these when the regrets are piled high

Sculpted into a statue made up of formative memorial debris

I sit back admiring the things used to shape my being and remember

It's time to love me

Comfort

Comfort used to soothe from the jukebox
Pulsing across my body in waves
Radiating through my brain, rattling the locks
Echoing up from within the deepest of mental caves

Leaving work meant abandoning the light
Battling a darkness swarming with fears
With no reinforcements, alone in the fight
Left to the courage found at the bottom of beers

Now it comes from the satisfying whistle of a kettle
The scent of peppermint wafts about the house
Competing with a candle, or flowers petal
Contentedness now a billowing flame I dare not douse

Having left behind the world of the bar
For a life of monumental happiness
Now and then rubbing the scar
Unbelievable, I used to think I deserved less

Bloom

People are plants or so I've been told
Needing water and sun on a timeline
Separated only by emotions, **Bold**
But I've never felt love from a pine

Is the language of the woods all its own?
Or could I learn it if I listened close?
Does the grass cry out when freshly mown?
Whispering a song of loss across the willow boughs

I've rejoiced while dancing in the rain
Feeling sadness pour from the gutters of my soul
Cleansed of remorse, doubt, and pain
Never thinking of the flowers fragile emotional control

How could I cast these things into the dirt?
Filling the world around me with gloom
How do they grow through the hurt?
Is there a chance I might still bloom?

Therapy

I have sat in that chair
When my emotions tried tearing my life apart
Humbled by the fact I was still sitting there
Questioning what made me worthy of a fresh start

Carrying anger, embarrassment, and guilt
Folded up neatly in a book bound in shame
I read from it now, within the temple my peers helped build
Knowing now, love can sprout from blame

If you're sitting in that chair
You are not sitting alone
It took me too long to learn
No matter how many times I was shown

I've stood in that room speaking in a hush
Afraid to upset who I thought was me
But that's who I am, it's who I was
And I would have never learned the difference, without therapy

Progress

Growth is not a line
Time doesn't heal all wounds
You just learn to acknowledge
To process every instance of "I'm fine"

The hurt can still collapse you
Lay you low
Buckle your knees without a "how do you do?"
Remember every one of those times
That is when you grow

Healing doesn't happen overnight
Your progress matters to me
I know how hard it is to be alone in this fight
Please remember how hard love is to see

I didn't believe it was with me at all
In the darkness I was plummeting through
But now that I've survived the fall
I can only hope you hear me screaming out to you

Amongst our darkest days, stories bloom. Together we will rise, embracing the strength in vulnerability.

I hope you can embrace the journey, and these words serve as a guiding force towards healing.

I've battled with depression and alcohol-rooted coping mechanisms for most of my adult life. It took getting a DUI in 2018 for me to realize I didn't know how to process my own emotions. Sure, I could suppress them long enough to forget momentarily, but I had no idea how to understand myself. I didn't know the "why"; I'd never put drinking down long enough to ask why. That's no way to live.

If any of the writing within this book resonates with you, I will consider this project an absolute victory. You are not alone, seeking help is not a weakness, and I believe in you.

Made in the USA
Middletown, DE
16 March 2024